MW00833788

WRITERS REPUBLIC

THE
UNDOING

ENTRIES OF ENCOUNTER

MEREDITH DIANNE O'NEAL

Copyright © 2021 by Meredith Dianne O'Neal.

All rights reserved. No part of this book may be reproduced in any form or by any electronic or mechanical means, including information storage and retrieval systems, without permission in writing from the publisher, except by reviewers, who may quote brief passages in a review.

This publication contains the opinions and ideas of its author. It is intended to provide helpful and informative material on the subjects addressed in the publication. The author and publisher specifically disclaim all responsibility for any liability, loss, or risk, personal or otherwise, which is incurred as a consequence, directly or indirectly, of the use and application of any of the contents of this book.

WRITERS REPUBLIC L.L.C.
515 Summit Ave. Unit R1
Union City, NJ 07087, USA

Website: *www.writersrepublic.com*
Hotline: *1-877-656-6838*
Email: *info@writersrepublic.com*

Ordering Information:
Quantity sales. Special discounts are available on quantity purchases by corporations, associations, and others. For details, contact the publisher at the address above.

Library of Congress Control Number: 2021953085
ISBN-13:   978-1-64620-968-2   [Paperback Edition]
                    978-1-64620-969-9   [Digital Edition]

Rev. date: 01/03/2021

Undoing: (noun)

an act of loosening; a cause of ruin.

Part I

Wisdom Is a Woman

I don't know who I am or where I am going. I turn twenty-three in a couple of weeks. I will be in treatment—learning, listening, resetting. Or I may be resettling into me—I like that better. She fits. I have wandered many ways and wounds to find myself here again, at the beginning of chapter 1. I am lost and found in the puzzle of sand that seeps through my flesh. A gentle mourning drizzle stained my pillowcase in gray. It was nice to let the windows open, their incarcerated cries have been muffled for very long. Today, I am sad inside. But I am glad the clouds let the water spill. The dream during the 2:00 a.m. thunderstorm taught me something—about how much pain my vessel has been holding on to, fearing exposure to the sunlight. My flower is sensitive to climate change. The water needs to be changed, the pottery needs to break. Her need is to cry, to breathe, and let the sunlight wrap its rays around the tender heart that beats within her.

Maybe the life our "Higher Power" is asking of us is not inner repression of the true self but rather the outer self. "Higher Power" is the living, breathing embodiment of the inner self. The inner self is rooted in the inner guide. The inner self, the Voice. The Voice is hard to hear. Even when the Voice whispers, we discard the pure vulnerability that reaches out towards us that is living beneath, through us. This occurs often, especially while the outer self is busy proving, projecting, and performing an unreachable, ever-changing, chaotic, turbulent, restless, standard of "perfectionism." I am starting to accept my inner self, slowly. It is a process of peeling back the layers of costumes of the outer self I have worn in order to be loved. To be loved, to be beloved, starts when I sit and listen to the inner self. The desires of the inner self were born shameless and naked. The inner self speaks what I desire and asks if I will honor it. What is desire? I am unwinding and unwrapping that lie now, in the present moment. Desire is not a dirty thing. Desire is the pivotal heartbeat. She is the blood that circulates through the soul of the inner self. My desire to be vulnerable, hurt, angry, seen, spirited, loved, needed, weak, shaken, messy, unapologetic, serving, compassionate, shameless, free, creative, expressive, is of the inner self. The inner self does not demand but rather invites the outer self into truth, recognition, and belonging. The inner self is patient and gentle, a guide to invitation. She never says no to extending open arms of abandoned ego towards the outer self.

Stop, breathe.

For love, for belonging is not based on attachment.
For love, for belonging is not based on achievement.
For love, for belonging is not based on acquisition.
For love, for belonging was.
For love, for belonging is.
For love, for belonging will be.
For love, for belonging cannot be stripped from me.
For love, for belonging cannot be stolen from me.
For love, for belonging is mine to receive.

Let it be intense. Let this be our mess. Let the pen pierce this paper with distinction—periods and new beginnings. Let the wet black hold nothing back. Do not apologize for need. You are showing up aware, staring at the faces of your emotions in sobriety. You are an honest heart, unashamed to start again. Show up for yourself dressed in graciousness, inviting your anxiousness to be embraced by unconditioned love.

The sweet sap of surrender;
The dripping dew of salvation.
Refreshment, glistening grace,
poured upon the pavement of my heart.

—*the rainy season*

Some thoughts from yesterday reminding me today...
"How beautiful would the world be if we celebrated our messiness? Compassionately gave ourselves permission to explore our errors without fear of retribution? Embraced negative self-language with kindness? Graciously wrapped our arms around insecurity? What if we dared to fall in love with the parts of us we deem undesirable and deficient? What if we willingly chose to be gentle towards our inner poverty? Maybe it would unite us. Maybe it would remind us that we are human.
Breathe, be generous with yourself today."

The muscle of divinity is found in the wood grains of surrendered strength, humility.

I surrender to this season.

Radiance is breaking through. It is the heart in you, darling. You are daring to love again.

The earth breathes.
The wind sings, a belting in the trees,
live lung's exhalation.
The humming hymns of riddling rhythms billow;
tambourine trees shimmer and shake as branch breaks.
I peer into the heavenly dimension.
Chest expression sets mind impressions.

If I lose humility, I lose everything.

And in a moment, the season can shift. And the season doesn't wait for you to catch up and figure it out. No, season merely extends an invitation, "Will you come along with me? Will you trust me amidst uncertainty?"

And as tears fell, he came intimately. His hands held my face.
I felt his humanity touch me. He drew water from my eye wells.
His lips kissed my skin. Trembling in beloved-ness
Concealed in nakedness, purified in the presence of being,
I am made...whole. His lips, soil to my skin, sprung flowers
wild in bloom.

Supported by the trees,
your hands imprint on me.
Out here with you, I can lay me down.
Arms like wings, you guide me.
Your substance is generous,
expansive, still, present. A paradox—
the break in the clouds of my purpose.
My weight does not intimidate you
but rather is invited to be washed
through and through.
You do not water me down
but rather unhinge my pretense.
I can finally be full.
Rest is found.
You sing into my form, softly,
movements in your speech.
It was you who taught my body to breathe.
My lungs and your limbs
will carry me, always.
You hold my fingers,
facilitating warmth and belonging.
You invite me into spacious,
and released from this cage named Anxious.
When I return, I believe
that this me can be supported by your trees.

Meredith Dianne O'Neal

Pervasive, persuasive—stay here
in the permanence of muck and mire
that plagues your weary soul to tire.
You'll survive, though your tubes are tied.
Bottled breath, what's left?
Bayou lungs gurgle gray water.
Cloggy cough sipped from the poisoned trough.
Wound clock, chest perspire,
induced by mind demon liars.

I wasn't created to survive,
I was created to live.

—Alive

At another's feet,
I surrender my need to be right,
with my need for a relationship.

—Loraine's wisdom

Fear is a teacher. Perhaps fear is an invitation to respond with honesty. Perhaps fear is a subtly entry, off-key, abrasive melody. Gallery, the exposition of need. Shipwrecked, abandonment of self-sufficiency. We have a limited supply of groceries. I am reminded of a gift—uncertainty. Rest does not delight in ignorance, dismissal, or apathy. Rather rest dances. Rest, trust falling in the present. May our lives be evenings, to lay down our gravel at another's feet. To be—to be stained by trials, rhythmic intention, belief. May uncertainty invite us to believe rest will make a way complete.

Red, yellow, and green
are traffic lights and trees.
The mechanic and the organic
are chosen as joinery.
The fall of coexistence,
a collection of fallen findings.
A canvas dressed in mess
and sown in grace.
At the sigh of the wind,
a scattered brain is rinsed with potion,
watercolor deliverance.
A posture of thanksgiving is a humble gain.
Still orange whispers, "Savor this season"
for a new pigment awaits around the book's bend.

Today, I bask in light of infirmity, a painted space around the splinter. The projection of our mind is a powerful source of trajectory. My mind is a world traveler, sailing on a boat in the desert. I try to make sense of this place. I often try to resurrect crumbs and scraps with a sponge, though this never seems to work. I am complexity, simplicity and infinity—a puzzle piece of depth, breadth, and momentary emotion. I take up space, and that is okay. I give myself the permission to throw away scarcity through surrender, simultaneously starting again.
I break my windowpane and invite breath to sing a lullaby
to my skeleton thoughts.

Remember to receive—
There is no fear in need.
It is never too late to start again.

In the deep of the undoing, I didn't eat much.
Dressed in deceit, killing, starving, felt filling.
My lips were dry. They cracked and bled.
My eyes were heavy, bruised with burdens.
I cried often. My spirit, sore.
My wings, wounded.
I thought about clipping them.
Anxious thoughts manifested into stomach knots.
Sadness rang its rags in my breast.
Black oil paint stained on my chest.
I tried to scream, but nothing came out.
Air was tight.
It was hard on my body to continue fighting.
Soul felt heavy, uneasy, and unsteady.
I wore black often and hid myself in thought coffins.

Your victory is not found in your armor attempt to "fight."
Your victory is found in your gravest unraveling—surrender.

Spring will come. The cherry blossoms say, "Spring will begin again." In your frantic panic, in your frenzied fear, you will find safety. Trust you have a friend near. Your heart alters matter. Dear friend, breath in, cast your anxiety out. Hold my hand, hope is near, this is not the end.

Pain is not the end. Hear me again: pain is not the end, dear friend. It is only the trek test through deeper dimensions. When you're ready to stop fighting, a haven is waiting for you. Rest resides there. The keeper cares.

Give yourself permission to cry. Unhinge your caged eyes and let your tributary truths fly.

The space of spontaneity is birthed in presence. A space where the pressure is taken off, and all is asked of you is to be.

People care about what you say,
But people care more about who's speaking—
Is it the voice of love or the voice of hate?

I show up. Awakened to messy entanglement, heartstrings. I breathe in bravery. A courageous child I was created to be.

—Dark room processing

The fearless flight. Stomach drops before the fall.
The surrender plunge. The hope net is awaiting to hold you.
"I've got your hand tightly gripped in mine. I'll wait until you're ready." And we run and we fall together. Undone by breath.
The brevity of *the Undoing*.

I give myself permission to break—

To process pain.
To hear fear.
To stare into the eyes of demons.
To face darkness.

Surrender fight,
surrender self-protection.
Surrender walls,
surrender self-defense.

Words are my freedom weapons.
I find myself here.

I laugh in the midst of unknowing. My laugh's name is Surrender.
Many things frustrate me in the midst of unknowing.
But this is good; it means I'm losing control. I find myself in
this foreign familiarity.

Grains of grace fill my heart space. Butterflies erupt and bloom
from the imprisoned room. This is the gardener's spout,
living water, seedling sprouts. Allergy hallelujahs prompt
the promised pollen. Soul's spring sings once again.

Today, I did something wild and free. I gave myself permission to be messy. I painted outside the lines of expectation and performance. I laughed at the stagnancy that used to suffocate me. Fear is a friend who invites you to peer into the darkness haunting you. Today, I choose my vindication dedication. Her name is Vulnerability.

The poverty of the soul is the best place to be whole. Empty: to be emptied, a metamorphic beholding. A scene of seeing true self, nakedness, and abundant benevolence. I am the beloved. I love insecurity. I befriend her and clothe her in kindness. I love pride. I befriend her and clothe her in compassion. Poverty is a child awakening a king in the dead of night for a glass of milk. Nourishment won't turn away.

Do I owe a penance for my presence? Shame is never satisfied. I will start now. Self-acceptance is the soil I choose to grow through. I will plant my mind in deep soil, self-compassion, and watch her germinate. I will speak in the foreign tongue, "I love you." And then perhaps one day, her breath will become her reality.

I dare you to fall in love with your inadequacy. This is a slow burn, a daily entry of engagement. Don't diminish your intensity; go on a walk in the sweltering heat. Write it down, accept all—the provocative and the neat. Speak up about your mental health, especially when you silence. Befriend your mind. Remember to breathe something kind. Give yourself permission to take up space. To embark is human all of the time.

I have much to speak but little to say. When I start writing, it will come out of me. What holiness is my hollowness? My nothingness is exceptional and extraordinary. My breath is triumphant. My lungs are air balloons. I am okay with who I am. I am okay with the layers that have been peeled backwards and forwards. I am okay with me—inhale and exhale all of me. May I ever be falling in love with her, her complex simplicity. May my webs be embraced with space and heart's blood veins. May my arms gather weeds and garden flowers all the same. I am amazed at the captivity and capacity you have birthed in the prison within my soul. Pain is the greatest paint to mark me.

I am okay with me, all of me.
I breathe, I am alive in me.
I have taken up residence
In the substance of my beloved-ness.
I once rented a shell space.
I left the cape in the closet.

Falsehood, you were once my escape. You are a part of me, that is much okay. There is much I would like to bestow upon you at the gracious table. Let me feed you with notice and nourishment.
I see you now, your screams now cease. Come child, linger in the light. You are safe, you are secure, you have always been loved far before the error. It is okay, you are okay with me.
I love you because without you, I would not have all of me.
I am beloved now, thank you for letting me go.

Rainy Thursday, how I love you.

Rainy Thursday, you write to me.

Rainy Thursday, you wet, wrinkle, and bleed.

Rainy Thursday, you strum my heartstrings and sing lullaby melodies to me.

Rainy Thursday, you whisper into my ear, "Invest in me."

Rainy Thursday, you rock me on your front porch under the eve.

Rainy Thursday, you place your hands on my heart and speak, "Beat."

Rainy Thursday, you pursue my messy humidity.

Rainy Thursday, you love me.

There is sorrow in the soul of the tree—an inclement day illuminates the tears in her chest. Cheeks chilled; the rush was blush. Tree, a sanctuary of depth and discovery. Her heart burns my skin; dense, deep, and wide is this gravity. Weighty is too heavy, it breaks her limbs and, like a slow burn, deteriorates the roots of the tree. Critters swarm, draining the nectar from her sacred leaves. Flowers wrinkling reach out once more, towards air and light, asking to be grazed by the palms of nourishment. She pleads, "I do not want to become a pressed, trapped, tree on the walls of the living."

I will not be the recipient of your pain.
I will not be the recipient of your punishment.

Your abuse is yours to heal, not mine to feel.
Your torture chamber is your imprisonment, not mine to conceal. You choose any form of vulnerability, a projector screen to pin the neck of your bloodshot eyes. You cry tears of blood. Rotting teeth and a crooked smile corner your undefiled. You rage, wolf. You mourn, child. Your wound is not mine to heal.

"Prison Wings"

Slave bleeds free. Wings are weeping through splinters and feathers. Let this intensity be found in whispers. Winter will deliver. My lips are a bow, quivering, whispering into the abyss. Gentle breath cradles innocence from death. Belonging starts in arms stretched like waves, staining crimson hands. Here you are held, between begin and end.

On the brink of balance and the chaos, let it be made.
I fear my own success. I would like to stay small, but growing
pains have their ways. Spacious is my return into the north.
I am ambition, dreams, and becoming.

Stretch marks are not glamorous, but truthful. Creating space in our skin is often an uncomfortable liberation. We are soiled and beautiful bruised fruit. Ripe and ruined. This is what healing looks like.

Conflict is costly, costly is conflict.
Suffering is buffering.
Waiting.
Anticipating.
Loading, zone pacing.
Though you may feel paralyzed by stagnancy,
the season is changing.
Present is tension, to be…a learning lesson.
Progress is resistance. An invitation to lovingly linger,
to embrace pain with kind.
Compassion, vine. I see the other side,
patience is your guide.
Strength training is mundane.
Threads are we, daily routine.
Risen bread reads in between.

I woke up craving substance. A cloud of illusive smoke and mirrors cannot satisfy me. It is not until I return to enter in the quiet that I see clearly. What was unseen but present in all? The nothing—substance, security, the patience of being. I was created for substance.

Eyes are intrusive—
leave thoughts, swirling lies, abusive.
Divorce, bruises.
To sink or to swim or to get drunk on a whim?
A ship adrift, who are you trying to please?
Measuring your prediction,
last night sails you into affliction.
Your audacity is exquisite.
You are off and magnificent.
You are misunderstood and alienated;
your greatest asset is this craft.
Despondence is elevated.
Stuffed to the bone, shivering isolation,
who is alone?
Melodramatic pause, empty avenue,
flickering lights, applause.
My artistry are my children.
Woven and messy, nothing unproven.
You are here in this to speak.
So go against the grain, abandon refrain,
speak straight regardless of interpretation,
projection, interaction.
Take up space in the caves of your bones, build, nest,
belonging is your bold.
Your life is here,
take a risk, you are home.

Part II

Lovers Lost and Found

Misty eyes, a wilting blush,
and canyon lips echo into me.
The end is titled *Beginning*.
Soft cotton soaked in violent passion.
"Recollect," the gravestone said.
A smeared oil "mine," tears, and rounded badlands,
mark me in *x*'s and *o*'s on our spot in the grass.
There is an eternity between this vein
and your concrete building in New York City,
a silver lining tightrope.
The clouds parted today, it started to water.
The sun has found me in Arizona, a desert contradiction
smeared in aloe butter and spaghetti-strap sunburn.
I must tell you, newly addicted is yours truly.
This white, burning, powder—Starlight.
She dances between deep-blue bedding,
twinkling, entangling my thoughts in her limbs.
The endangered, warm stain asks me to stay.
A wooden beam emerges from her throat.
Splinters in my toes, creaking floors, and panty hose.
I stay. I show her that love
is not meant to be given like this and thrown away,
like yesterday's Chinese take-out.
Recall that place you took me to?
In the Bronx, sandwiched between the deli
and the Sal's convenience store?
I am writing to tell you my latest insights.
Enjoy your life in the Big Apple,
I hope the cold keeps you young and pretty.
XO, the last foreign lover.

Meredith Dianne O'Neal

Sandpaper lips skim her skin.
Bones are a violet dusk. Sun's kiss, orange-rouge
paints her roof. Dusk paves a path
Unframed portrait.
Treasure chest, desert plain.
Chamber houses pain.
May refrain from explanation.
Learning lesions.
Pressed petals sympathize
with invisible bruises. Pigments undignified.
Storm eye rains, watercolor cries.
May, a love letter.
Her typewriter snivels. Her ink simmers.
Sinking teeth, crème bliss, he delivers.
A mist, an abyss. Cheeks, stovetop.
Fingerprints sew blood clots.
Mind quake, tremors.
Falling leaves, trapped hair.
Pressure, pleasure.
Frame is a jaded edge, remember.

Stripped back, strip down,
like an orange peel that hits the ground.
This was what it was like loving you,
taking off layers of my clothing.
First my jean jacket, then my white T-shirt.
Bare chest, mountains, and valleys
that I invited your adventure into.
It was never just skin,
I let you eat the rawest and rarest of my meat.
Here we are again, meeting on the green bench in the park.
"Working through" because you asked me to.
We rewind the mixed tape and pretend that it's fate.
I let you in because you knocked
Showed up with flowers in hand,
Lilies, my favorite. Fragrant and ripe.
Yet, you were sour to the bite.
A "happy" ending without a chorus or melody.
Blank stares and frozen lips.
Illusions and reflections seemed
to mend my mind's idea of "perfection."
Come down from the sky,
come close, let's take a hike.
Here you are again, in the mountains and valleys,
you once invited others into.
Yet this love story was always about loving you.

The invincible summer,
high on sunlight listening to "6s to 9s."
Glistening back, crisp bacon stove lines.
You and me, windows down
belting the eclectic kind, freedom melody.
Starry, starry night and strobe lights.
Darkness and light coexist
in a studio apartment for a moment in flight.
Dance floors, sore feet, hangovers, and late brunch
with plentiful croissants, tart fruits, and sincere regrets.
Butter me up in tanning oil,
blue waves with fleshly refrain,
float on and contemplate.
Mountaintop, crisp air, weed, and a hint of pine.
Dry skin in mine looking for lotion
to resurrect your source of contempt.
A pitched tent, dog barks, and black coffee.
Return to the campsite.
Go back, let her go,
golden knotted hair wove a crown out of her bow.
Her indie spirit will flow in the wind.
A flag is cast within.
Do not forget again,
summer "her" is only a passing show.

I can't open the well, it's dry,
how will I nourish her now?
You know her well,
the pit under the breast where you'd
occasionally throw your change into me.
Cracking under pressure,
leafy growing around my extremity.
Vines and breeze, rich wine coursing
through my river blues.
Hesitation rushing in,
a flag waving on the clothesline.
Lingering hold on the asphalt street.
Feet are grounded for a present unwrapping.
Life is in motion, fumes, and piles of clothes.
A planking floor, and a night before.
I am homesick for the "what ifs", hung up like my keys.
Checkmate makes your move against the door.
Darling, don't you know,
the thought of us makes me sore.

Wet dew, overdue. Under the moon,
to see clearly is looking back at you.
We are infinite, like your sugar skin soaking in.
I want the forest pines on your arms
and the whirlpool in your kaleidoscope eyes.
I want to absorb you, adore you.
Suckle the sweetness from your crop.
The sun will come up soon.
We are infinite; your femininity
makes my mouth water.
Beneath the expanse, "I'll never leave you...,"
The night-light said to the fortitude.
Draw near to pastel, then withdraw into solitude.
It's okay to like flowers, I like flowers too.

Black butterfly, you are a silent scream.
Black butterfly, you are a jaded delicacy.
Black butterfly, you smear your weak.
Black butterfly, you are blue velvet ink.
Black butterfly, you are a haunting beauty.
Black butterfly, you are masked in moody.
Black butterfly, your wings whimper.
Black butterfly, your glass stains dimmer.
Black butterfly, your flutter is a tremor.
Black butterfly, you are the limbs of December.
Black butterfly, why do you land on me?
Black butterfly, why do you dress me in despair?
Black butterfly, do your pigments even care?

Gouache gloom, won't you wash over me
in happenings and new beginnings?
Giddy schoolgirl with a sugar rush
as big as her crush.
I feel the butterfly cage in my belly,
the warm glow under my covers.
I see you now but can't have you.
You are a distant figure in plain sight.
Distance is a good thing,
I think. Stay in my lane, but daydream
brings me to your bed.
Curled up in crème with black
brewing in the teal kitchen.
At least I have the words to get you
out of my chest.
So that I don't have to hold on
to the possibility of a distant daydream,
that after all is a daydream.

Reclaimed Scenes

Reach out to reach in,
fingers in my jam at the picnic again.
Lips like syrup to the bite,
candy apple and strawberry sun.
Together again, I thought I'd won.
"Sticky," you whisper.
I should have seen the sign in the rearview, "Run."
Your arrogance shows up unannounced and drunk by noon.
Foolishness and fleeting "pick-me-ups" became your tools.
Your mouth is wide open, like the ocean tide ready to consume.
A kid with no self-control
stuffing his face with a plastic spoon.
Superficial yet cool.
Candy cane, candy cone,
A whiskey sour kiss, then you take me home.
You are hungry, drooling over crumbs.
Prison walls have made you numb.
Searching again to be resurrected
and one day "become."
Success is in shortage.
Scarcity is your mortgage.
My accent wall you'd like to claim
for an empty house and an insecure ego.

Meredith Dianne O'Neal

Sing me to sleep in the big navy sheet, a whimper is in your disguise.
This twisted vine you wrap around my thigh, is quite discrete.
Blurry skies, watching the time pass by were up for keeps.
You taught me to choose.
A lesson learned and a heart earned, highlighted my need to choose abundance and new beginnings. Here, I leave behind your cheap tricks to another victim recipe.
Kiss, kiss, Burning Scenes, c'est la vie.

She is reliant on defiance.
She makes an alliance with isolation.
Striking and provoking,
thoughts often convulsing.
She is a sag petal.
She is excavating, sifting, and decomposing.
Destination varies,
words are always speaking.
She is intense relief, heavy breath, and sunken teeth.
Casing is claustrophobic,
Allergic to constriction,
Art is relieving.
Her chosen medium,
Words are her breakfast.
A relatively balanced diet.
She is okay with artistry.
She is unfolding the crinkled skin
that lies beneath her whim.
She is intense if she cares for you deeply,
eyes tell a story of unearthing.
She doesn't mind letting you in,
if you choose to linger.
She desires to be sought and seen,
to bloom in between the buildings.
The secret self that is learning to feed,
to nourish the heart with gentleness.
She bathes in compassion.
She cuts her pain with love.
She severs her fear with kind.
Comfort is the bedding of her mind.

Paint my lips in baby cool
and pray that I "miss you too."
Smile is a charmed view, routine and wild—
if there can be such a thing.
What the fuck am I saying?
Screaming but denial of fantasy.
I am afraid to live, but too am falling for a bad boy
in dark leather with an effective gaze.
Brain matters have been digging for buried treasure.
What is the purpose after Mother Earth awakes?
She is excavating,
pencil often breaks.
Her ocean is nauseous.
Her hair waves.
Seaweed washes up on the shore of her chest.
Braids, rope for her boat
and a mind lost at sea.
A mirage, a mystery dressed in blues,
an evening gown, and some sample carmine.
She glistens in depression,
haven't you learned "faking" is like eating cake?
Spongy and sweet yet adds weight
that it gets too heavy to breathe.
The birds are singing
through the cavities in her teeth.
Dull rage has gotten so normal
it sounds like "retreat."
Kitchen plates are falling from the shelves,
her limbs are slow to the rush.
She steps into the shatter and bleeds.
Punctured lung, but somehow, heart slow, still beats.

Amber wood, fireflies to sky
burning an ode of "once upon a time."
A poetic proposition—
black nails hold the kill, a grave between teeth.
"Thrill," you say,
"This is my choice, to destroy or reclaim."
Yellow lantern moon,
you leave me beneath the blanket sky.
Tears on my cheek, curves on the earth like dew.
Lungs like trees, howling for you.
Full moon, poker face.
Body out here in wide open space.
Far away and almost far gone.
Hold me tight and don't forget,
dawn has not placed her bet quite yet.

Climb up the tree that we planted
in play and innocence.
I feel angry now. You burnt my tree down,
watered passions down with a gardening hose.
You destroyed innocence with ignorance.
Fuck you.
Extreme in me bridges passivity in you.
Do you see? I hold a fire in my palms,
embers that once grazed you.
Suddenly, an ember was conceived
in the night sky.
Red laced with chilled hues,
we named her *Alive*.

The trimmed shrubs are screaming within.
They suffocate, stuck in the
conformity cycle of broken china.
Let them breathe.
Let their growth enter into
the edge of eternity.
Let them run into the mother's field
without the tragedy of visibility.
No harness on the free horse in me.
Free me from the hungry grip,
Greedy, bloody fingers are a liability.
I scream and shout from a dry spout,
there is breath in the bombardment.
Wells of wishful thinking, I find myself daydreaming.

Build me up and then tear me down,
like the house for sale on the corner.
The one with the dormer windows,
with the angles shaped like slight frowns.
Go down to the river,
undress yourself, before that cut lip
speaks into your reflection.
Curse words and flashy red heels
were my culprits as I tripped down your hill.
You were in love with me, remember?
Your "firefly ember" that lit your face up
like a kid on the playground. You cared.
Oh hell. What am I now, but clogged hair in the drain?
I have fallen out, but somehow dally in the remains.
Shriveled, dry, thirsty for your pigments on my canvas.
Resurrect me with your bare hands.
I want your lips in forbidden places,
mark my cave walls and crevasses.
Sink your teeth into my canyon,
plant a stream, expand me again, and again.
You set up camp before the quake,
then you abandoned it.
The moonlight of your eyes,
soft cream to this dark scene.
I want you to touch me with your fragility.
Sow me, won't you?
On the machine, the merry-go-round that built "we."
Hurry, before I throw up from the dull sirens
calling me to "fucking grow up."
I guess I loved you.
The "guess" is a gesture of my affection.
Take it as a compliment.

A stain of love like this cannot be contained.
This blood type is rare.
We, the seesaw in the yard.
The candy store forget the effects
of sugar on the stomach.
We ignore the ache and take shots, straight.
The original crown moldings make us want "more."
Thin sweat beads my neck.
"Pearls are made in tension," you said.
You pull my hips close and "borrow" a dose.
How I've become an addict of Chanel eyeliner
and dancing shadows in the back of yellow cabs.
The streetlights paint my sight in silver strokes.
A momentary pastel, where you and I are
briefly held in the arms of a backyard Kodak memory.
Upgraded, we live in the Upper East Side now.
A city loft, where people say we live "comfortably,"
Yet this is an anomaly.
Relocated, to see if another city could light a match
in this vacant house.
What Neiman's skin care regimen
can heal these scars now?
Running away, but running into you.
A stain of love like this cannot be contained.
To hold on or to let it go,
but don't you already know?
No designer handbag can sew a hole this big and bold.

It pains me to press the pen.
But I need to in order to survive.
The shower is running warm.
Rushing down my back
like a rock waterfall in a far-off place.
I am close, but at arm's length.
Paradise is rarely found
but, in your stroke, left on the wall.
Distraction has become enthralling.
Will I get to a place where I want to live?
Scratch the skin off my back
like a snake shedding last season.
Night has become comforting,
darkness encompassing.
Shadows drift through the blinds
like a tipsy woman speaking in slur.
Everything feels prickly and blurry.
Everything feels—body, mind, embrace.
What will I do with the remains?
Stain my face in oils
that will take forever to dry.
The student and teacher are one and the same.
Night, though familiar, is like day,
kicking and screaming in silent dissonance.
Sarcastic and cynical, a broken tea set is critical.
I am bruised and drenched in lowlight,
paint floods my lungs, my brain.
I cannot see straight.
Sinking slowly into the depths of sand,

I am buried in memory and brilliance.
Strike while the iron's hot.
Ice-cold and fuming, the kettle does not know
the likeness of the room temperature economy.

Everything is so fucking intrusive and distant.
Maybe that's a part of the diagnosis.
The poison we keep on drinking like our morning coffee.
Nothing against coffee; like anyone, I am an addict
of somebody or something.
I wish a lot, pennies in the dry well
that reflect in the sun and somehow show the edge
of my jaw line or the bones that built my body's frame.
More than half the time, I have no idea
what I am saying, but the clock
is in fact delayed. Like most things,
a delayed response is rather ineffective
and accepted these days.
Everything feels dry and fragrant.
I don't know how,
so please don't ask me why!
For some odd instance, I feel like
a dead man living, consoled in
pillow talk, riddles like this.
They tuck me in for the evening,
then unwind me, find me,
in a unique deliverance.
The life I've lived is nothing like I expected,
and what a fantastical gift indeed.
To be fucked up, somewhat broken,
yet moving forward and feeling every damn thing.
This must be what it means to be alive.

For a long while, I was looking for you,
When truly, I was looking for me too.
You whispered; I have to "let in…in order…to let go."
I am frustrated and frazzled.
Split ends and bruises on my knees.
I thought you wanted real,
here she is indeed.
I hear a beat outside of my window
that has me questioning the words to a melody.
I am frightened and scared by what is coming.
It is not spooky, but revealing,
my innards are falling out of me,
like rose petals on the harshest of realities,
the charcoal pavement.
A piece of my organs,
necessities for the picnic.
Rich jam for your bread
is washed away by the summer rains.
Dirt is smeared on the streets of the city,
like the foundation running down my face.
I cry sometimes, wipe my eyes with my sleeve,
sinking into the cushion chasm.
Bleeding is vibrant, but silent.
Pray in a rosy lip that no one will see.
My shriek is hidden in the unworked hands
of my own belongings.
Hills and valleys where vulnerability touched me
woke me up in a cold sweat from the heat.
I cannot look away from the reflection
that pierces into me, honestly.
She is all I ever asked for, *honesty.*
But sometimes, I wish the music would stop.

Meredith Dianne O'Neal

I wish the clock would take a break from ticking.
I wish many things—what is worth wishing?
The beat is agitating.
My nails have been filed by my teeth.
This is what unbecoming has led me to.

Summer sick, if there is such a thing.
Hung over on the absorption of activity.
Social antiquity, a star-lit porch
is a perfect place for us—tragedy.
Who am I? Why does my desert skin shiver and shed?
Your fingers play my instrument,
a name unspoken in the light.
Am I unsure of this?
My exhibit is open, a scattered mind
and lip-stained mirror.
I am losing it in the stillness between us two.
Gravity sways and spins
my spider legs around the room.
I am dehydrated, I am intoxicated by you.
Summer lover, summer blue,
summer sick, summer you.

CPSIA information can be obtained
at www.ICGtesting.com
Printed in the USA
LVHW011914300122
709653LV00003B/86